# Mud Pies

MW01242380

*A Merry Mixture of Memories*

by Kathy Poss Little

## Table of Contents:

# Preface

Travel with me as we journey back in time to the 1950s and 60s.
Within these pages I share vivid memories in stories, poems and
pictures of my life growing up in a rural Georgia community. A few
stories are more recent and reflect life in South Carolina.
My life as a country girl was uncomplicated and carefree. My intent
is not to burden the reader with a dreary recollection of hardships
that every family faces. Rather, I offer a glimpse into small events
and situations chock full of the elements that make life good.
Mostly, this is a happy book of simple everyday occurrences.

*~ Kathy's Childhood Home ~*

Here you will find a well-traveled journey of self-discovery and character building. Fondly looking back, my appreciation grows everyday for all I have received from kindhearted, loving people. Although we were far from rich monetarily; family, friends and community were so caring and warm that I never really noticed. In a subtle way my upbringing felt grand and glorious.

This written account brings life to a time that is quickly fading. May these poems and brief stories interest and amuse you. I thank God for wonderful people who inspired me with lasting impressions and sprinkled my life with laughter and love.

I wish for you a life journey full to the brim with a mixture of magical moments and merry memories.

Kathy Poss Little

# 1) Happy Birthday Baby

Celebrations of life roll around every year. If we are still young, we want to be older. If old, we wish to be younger and have all the characteristics of the young.

At 16 we are sweet, at 18 we are ready to graduate from school, and tackle the world. At 21 we have to prove we are adult. At 50 we talk about being 40. Being called "middle aged" is a surprise the first time it's heard. At 60 we hear "mam and sir", a reminder we are now senior citizens. At 70 we begin to think about what 80 may be like. At 80 we want a clear mind and a healthy body to continue enjoyment of life. We have arrived, but where? Where have we been? Did we go too far? Did we stop before we were finished? Did we go the way of "should" or did we live outside the box? The unknown waits for our signals and our direction.

There was a man who didn't live by the rules of the majority. He was Lendsey Lanier Poss. Somewhere along the way he was given the nick-name "Pete" and was so fond of it; he removed his middle name, Lanier, from his birth certificate and changed legally to Pete. Lendsey Lanier's birthday was May 9, 1918. He made it through the 6th grade but finished his learning working from sun up till sun down tilling the soil and doing whatever was needed to help his family. He joined the Army and went off to war leaving behind his sweetheart, Lois Clotilde Ivey. Letters were received often by his mother and sweetheart. Pete was discharged from the war, honorably, and soon married Clotilde. Six years passed and his daughter arrived.

~*Mildred Kathleene Poss and Lindsey Pete Poss*~

Born on her Daddy's birthday. Mildred Kathleen's birthday was May 9, 1950. Pete was 32 that very day. He was excited after a long awaited child, he could barely think of anything else. When the doctor announced that Clotilde was fine, and that he was the father of a healthy, beautiful baby girl, he took a breath and sighed with relief. He was so proud, so honored to be a father. He enjoyed smoking his cigars and had a couple in his pocket to give away exclaiming his joy. His baby girl, his first born, was his birthday gift. Years went by, and with each birthday there was a double celebration. Their love deepened. The bond became stronger between father and daughter, unspoken and almost inexplicable. Each year, as the joint birthday approached, Pete would ask Kathy,

"How old are we this year"? Laughter would ensue because whatever age Kathy was, Pete was just as young and vibrant! No doubt it was his way of honoring his daughter, her youth and his appreciation of life.

*~Mildred Kathleene Poss~*

Pete enjoyed his birthdays, being just as silly as his young daughter but he was not a man to put up with too much tomfoolery. He claimed never to go to church every Sunday lest he become a hypocrite. He might drink a little on an occasional Sunday, but during the week he took his responsibilities seriously. Pete always provided for and took good care of his wife, children and mother who lived in the same house with them. He never let a day go by without saying "I love you" to each immediate family member. He was a little brother to two older sisters, and they came to visit during the week and weekends to see their mother Lucy. He loved them dearly, but if they tried to tell him what to do, or how to live, he would have nothing to do with it. Pete was an uncomplicated man sprinkling laughter often. He enjoyed his beagle dogs, pigs, and his outside work shop.  He spent many hours tinkering on automobiles and trucks. He took pride in re-selling cars and trucks after refurbishing the engines and re-painting the body.

Birthdays for Pete were gentle reminders of a good life.  Kathy and Pete's joint
celebrations were usually private and at home, with a homemade, decorated cake and  ice cream. They made separate wishes and blew out the candles together. After Kathy married and left home, she missed those special times with her Daddy Pete. There were telephone conversations often and especially each May with happy birthday cheer.  Pete again asking Kathy, "How old are we today?" Kathy doesn't remember Pete talking about getting old.  He took life one day at a time and enjoyed the journey as best he could. He died so young, only 66, but it matters not how long we live, but how well we live. It's the fun and uncomplicated things that remain in the memory of the heart – shared birthdays and saying, "I love you". Heartstrings never break.

# 2) The Easter Egg Hunt

Easter was a holiday of much excitement. The Saturday before Easter, children and their parents gathered for a midday party and egg hunt on the church grounds. Sandwiches, cupcakes and candies were served to delight any child.

The eve brought anticipation of wearing a new dress, hat and shoes the following morning for church service. The Easter Bunny hopped by during the night and filled empty baskets with small surprises. Gifts could be a chocolate bunny, and a new box of crayons with coloring book. There was always something practical in the basket too; white socks trimmed in lace for the girls and maybe a pretty arm bracelet.

After church, lunch at home was eaten with haste so that all would be ready when the cousins arrived mid afternoon for the BIG Easter egg hunt. Please don't let it rain for we must hide lots of eggs today. Relatives arrived, baskets filled with dyed hen eggs in all colors of the rainbow. Girls came in pretty dresses with flowers, hats with ribbons and lace and shinny patten leather shoes. Boys wore white shirts, bow ties and dress pants.

The dinning room table was covered with baskets. It was a sight to behold with the egg count of two hundred and more. A favorite was the candy eggs wrapped in crispy cellophane to protect the hard candy coating and soft marshmallow center.

The eggs were hidden carefully among the rows of daffodils, under the pecan tree covered up with leaves and on the limbs of the trees. The glorious mimosa tree is noticed as it gently swayed with the wind, allowing the soft lilac blooms to deliver sweet fragrance through the air.

Children were running back and forth, filling baskets to the brim. Where is the golden prize egg? It is hidden well. The prize winner gets a large chocolate bunny, with a candy yellow bow tie and bright blue eyes.

The hunt is now over and children are exhausted. Removing their hats and shoes, they plop on the ground, eating eggs and candy as they wiggle their toes in the grass. The eggs must be counted. Ahh, some are missing. They must hunt again to find the last one before the day is done. What joy it's been to laugh and play, on this another grand Easter holiday.

~*Millicent Spring Barney*~

# 3) God In My Pocket

Going to church in the 1950s and 1960s was as much of a necessity as it was a choice. It was the heart and life of southern country community families. Services were every Sunday morning and evening. Monday just didn't feel right if church was missed. Staying home was only allowed for illness. No other excuses were acceptable. From the church family came true friends, the kind that gives comfort in trying times and laughter in happy times. The church was a place of activity and fun events for the community where the importance and value of life was shared and lived. Bethany Methodist Church was nestled in the wood, in a little corner of Lincolnton, GA.

Mother made sure we attended every Sunday at 10 o'clock sharp for the opening celebration and Sunday School Class. Congregants gathered in the sanctuary and then to rooms for class study of the Bible. One teacher I especially remember was Mrs. Cehoy Spires. She was beautiful with her lily white skin and dark shiny hair. Her kind gentle voice came with a smile. Stories she told from the Bible came to life. We were taught to believe in miracles, and to depend on God to be with us no matter what. My concept of God was vague in my younger years, but if God could make me kind and sweet like Miss Cehoy, then I wanted to learn more. The loud preaching from the pulpit gave a different and fearful impression of God. God is love, they would say, but also God might punish if we did wrong or bad things. They warned, God is always watching and he knows if you've been good or bad.

It was difficult for me to pronounce Miss Cehoy's name. It came out as "Miss See Soy". Daddy laughed when I pronounced it. In class she said God is everywhere. A curious boy asked if God was in our pocket. Miss See Soy confirmed, "God is everywhere even in your pocket". Hearing this news put me in a state of wonderment. I left the service questioning why powerful, all knowing God would ever want to be in the pocket of someone's clothing. The curiosity of it stayed in my thoughts. It was that very Sunday I had an awakening of the greatness of God. This was the beginning of my spiritual journey. I became much more attentive in church. I wanted to learn more about this heavenly, unseen being.

After classes all gathered in the sanctuary again at 10:45 A.M. for closing remarks and the benediction. There were announcements, and several songs from the hymnal. Since the paid minister was shared with two other churches, our "preaching service" was just once a month, occasionally twice. The minister was invited to someone's home for Sunday dinner, right after the service, pre-arranged from names on a list. Beforehand a date was set for the visiting preacher so that each family could prepare ahead of time and everything would be done just right. On Saturday before this important visit, the house was cleaned extra well. China almost never used except at Thanksgiving and Christmas, was taken out of the cabinet and dusted. Silver flatware was also used for the fine dining experience. Each piece had to be rubbed and polished with a soft cloth. Mother spent several hours on Saturday cooking wonderful food dishes and desserts that would please a king. I was warned and reminded how to act during the visit. A bit of nervousness was felt anticipating the preacher visit. Eventually I realized preachers and their families are just like the rest of us. They didn't have super powers as I had conjured up in my head.
Our best clothes were worn to church services. Paten leather shoes in shiny white or black were a staple. I especially enjoyed Easter, because we dressed up as if we were going to be in a grand parade. A couple of weeks prior to Easter, my parents drove us to the J.C. Penny Store in Augusta, GA to purchase new dresses. It was great delight looking through a wardrobe of beautiful dresses in pastel colors with lace or ruffles. Many dresses were trimmed with a satin sash tied in a bow to flow down the back of the dress. It was best to complete the outfit with a hat in white or matching pastel colors; adorned with tiny flowers and bows. A matching purse to accent the dress and paten shoes was the final touch. I felt so pretty when I put on the complete outfit. I was a princess for that one special day of the year.

At the end of Sunday church services the adults greeted each other with small talk while the children played. Mr. Edgar Albea, an older gentleman was a familiar face and I saw him every Sunday. He looked like a preacher himself with his dark suit, tie, and nice felt hat. He tipped his hat to the side when greeting the ladies. He had special gifts tucked in his coat pockets to give away to children. Calling us by name he put half pieces of chewing gum in our outstretched hand. Tutie-frutie was his favorite flavor. If it was the fall of the year he toted a bag of fresh pecans and handed 2 or 3 to each child. He was very kind and generous and won a place in my heart.

Many preachers of the gospel came and went over the years, but I knew I could count on Miss Cehoy and Mr. Edgar being there, good shepherds of the flock. Little did they know their kindness and service in our church was also molding young minds and hearts. Other than my parents and grandmothers, they were my role models. Learning to sing at church was very important. We used a hymnal that was passed down through the ages. I often wondered if I would ever be worthy enough to "walk the streets of gold" as one song suggested. The children learned special songs that were performed in front of the congregation. We stood in rows, with the tallest and oldest on the back and staggered down to the smallest of the children. One song still rings in my heart and is still sung in many churches, "There is a Joy". A line in one of the verses is "a peace that passes understanding". Until I was older and read the words for myself I was sure the words were "there is a piece of plastic understanding, down in my heart". I often wondered about the meaning of that line, but I sang it loud and with confidence. Our group of children was large, about 15 or 20. Someone must have noticed how beautifully we sang, and made an arrangement for a TV appearance. At six years old I traveled with the group to Augusta, GA to WRDW-Channel 12 for a show. Pictures were taken and we were in the local newspaper with the group picture and an article. Could this have been the start of a movie star career?

Summer vacation was just the right time to attend church and spend a week at Bible School learning more about God. There was much fun to be had as well with a mid-break in the day to have cookies, kool-aid and to play games. Drop the handkerchief, Red Rover, and Farmer in the Dale were just a few group games we played together.

With God in my pocket at the age of six came a sudden realization and a glimpse of the greatness and grander of a God filled life of wonder and magnificence. I have never forgotten those days and now realize the significance of my early church years.

~Bethany Church Sunday School 1956~

*~Bethany Church in Lincolnton, GA~*

# 4) Night Sky and Cool Grass

Summer evening was wrapping her arms around me; the cool mist kissed my skin. The damp grass felt cool and smelled sweet as I rolled in the grass on the knoll in the backyard. The uncut grass wrapped over my toes like a blanket. The sky was aglow with the soft velvety blue of the clear day and a blending of stunning pink as the sunset ushered in the evening. Earthy sweet smells filled the country air while soft breezes brushed my cheeks. The night sky was stunning as it danced softly with the artist pallet of swirling colors. Dew nourished the ground and every blade of grass welcomed it. Misty humid air was resting on my face and arms and I listened to sounds of night insects as they sang. Looking up at the stunning but softening sky, thoughts wondered and became hazy as my mind took in the entire universe. There was complete enjoyment in these pleasant private moments, just me and my universe. Fully appreciating the moment, nothing else mattered. My soul was fed, and my being was sustained. This was the place in mind and heart where dreams were nourished and miracles were believed. This was a calming experience and a gift for the ending of a delightful day. Let this place of peace go on forever. Let me stay. A familiar voice called, and pulled me back to my senses. It was Mother bidding me to come in for the evening.

Hesitating for another few minutes, looking around one more time as night crawled in darker and darker. There was an enticing feeling of safety. With another deep sigh I bid farewell to the earth and sky. You will be in my dreams tonight and I will see you again tomorrow. Goodnight. Walking away there was realization of reality, but the soul knows where to find this place of truth and purity again.

*~Lois Clotilde Poss with Kathy in 1954~*

# 5) The Turquoise Bicycle

Nineteen Fifty-Seven was a year with extra special gifts. Rose Mary Poss, my sister, was born in October. As if that wasn't exciting enough, December rolled around with another big surprise. Christmas morning I awakened with great expectations of a child who knew, beyond a doubt, that a certain roly-poly gentleman, with a flowing white beard, had visited during the night. I could almost hear his hearty laugh resounding about the room. Of course, I thought, he had deposited my dream-of-dreams beneath our bejeweled, family Christmas tree. I put on my robe and slippers, full of anticipation and joy. I headed toward the front of the house as rapidly as my feet would move. As I grew closer, I began to creep towards the living room, uncertain as to what was around the corner. I peeked with caution as if something dangerous was lurking about. At that moment the suspense gave way to a smidge of doubt. Then I caught a glimpse of my most favorite color. It was something turquoise. As it came into focus, my heart jumped. Could my dreams come true? There it was, the shiniest, and most beautiful turquoise bicycle I had ever seen. It surpassed my dreams. It took my breath away. I jumped with joy and rushed to touch it so I could be sure it was real. With a sigh of satisfaction, I gently rubbed the chrome as if to cautiously apply a thin coat of precious oil. It is mine, and it's my favorite color. It was love at first sight. It was the best Christmas ever.

It was so cold and rainy that particular December that I didn't want to take my prize out in that awful weather. I wasn't sure I could ride it. With spring approaching the weather warmed and it was time for me and my newest best friend, my bicycle, to share many new adventures. It had to be very easy learning to ride the bike, I thought. Friends learned and rode with apparent ease. Straddling the bike, both feet planted on the ground, hands ready on the handle bars, I froze. What next, NO idea. Panic struck, I tried to shove off with one foot on the pedal, but it wasn't happening. In frustration, more fear welled up. I gave up; knowing that tomorrow would bring victory. Many days passed with determined effort but with no success.   Shame and frustration mounted as each failure came.

Finally, after almost too much failure to bear, I went to my parents for help. They offered to push me off, staying near and promised I would stay balanced; being scared, I refused. They told me I had to be smarter than the bike. Clearly the understanding and indications of what that meant, was not helping. Suddenly the light dawned, and it was clear to me that it was going to take pure determination and positive self talk to get me in the right place to ride my turquoise wonder. Breaking in my wild horse would happen, and we would be forever friends. As helplessness turned into focus and courage, I knew everything would be alright. With inspired new energy and drive and in an almost trance like state of confidence - I took off. Riding, sailing, feeling the wind brushing across my face. I was free. I had finally won the fear battle.

In those few eventful weeks, I learned valuable lessons about life, self-belief, determination, overcoming frustration, perseverance, and focus.

While having a new baby sister was amazing, learning to ride my bike was the beginning of self mastery and faith. I had conquered myself. I had trampled on fear and earned self confidence. The turquoise bicycle was my cherished friend for years and still a reminder of an early lesson in courage and perseverance.

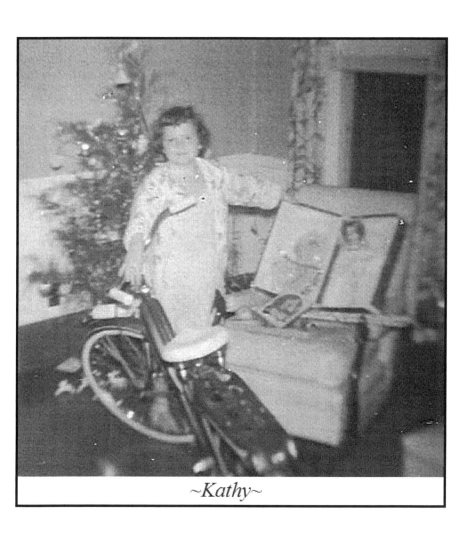

*~Kathy~*

# 6) THE WELL IS DRY

No water today.

We're in dismay.

Water well is dry…..

Mama Ivey wants to cry.

Water for cooking and for bath;

An outdoor spigot neighbor Clyde hath.

Gallon plastic jugs to use;

A request to fill, he cannot refuse.

Galvanized buckets too,

So silver they are almost blue.

A walking we must go.

Down a dirt road two and fro.

Dry, hot dirt between our toes,

Dusty feet and dusty clothes.

Kicking stones,

Stumping our toes.

Feeling the sun on our heads,

Singing a song -- roses are red.

The spigot outside comes into view,

Gardenias we pick and hyacinths of blue.

Scent of wet dirt as water trickles on dry soil,

Bucket full brim, the walk back is toil.

A cat purrs at our feet rolling in the grass,

Looking down we see a shiny piece of glass.

Time to go it's getting late,

A surprise at the house waits.

Smell of tea cakes in the air,

Hurry to open the screen door when we get there.

Mama Ivey takes a jug to the stove, pouring water into the pot,

Potatoes need cooking until they are good and hot.

Water buckets are placed on the back porch at the galvanized tub,

Later it's for bath and a good scrub.

We will dance and pray so that rain comes soon,

There may be water in the well again by day after tomorrow noon.

*~Mildred Ivey and Kathy~*

## 7) Chinaberry Soup and Mud Pies

Chinaberry trees grow tall and are of the mahogany family. It's native to Asia and Australia, bearing fragrant lilac flowers and yellow berries. It became naturalized in parts of North America. I knew of a grand Chinaberry tree when I was a child in our back yard in Lincolnton, Georgia. It gave wonderful shade where family and friends spent many happy hours beneath its branches cascading down in umbrella fashion. The bright green berries hung in clusters and eventually turned yellow before falling to the ground.

When my childish imagination took hold; it wasn't visions of lollipops that danced in my head. It was the fascinating fruit of the Chinaberry tree. There was caution issued that the appetizing berries would surely cause unwanted stomach pain if eaten. The warning of "don't eat the berries" only made for more curiosity. I popped one in my mouth when no one was looking. The bitter taste wrenched my face and caused me to shiver. I couldn't spit it out fast enough. That awful taste must have been nature's way of protecting little children from gobbling up those pretty berries. While the berries were not to be put in any food group, they did however have several playful uses.

During a short time period in the summer, the berries fell to the ground with every breeze. Some fell while still green, but most were yellow and ripe. I soon found out that running over them with the tire of my tri-cycle would create a sharp "popping sound". This took precision, skill, and focus to get the tire to run over a berry in just the right manner. This game would be the highlight of a pleasant morning.

During a day of whimsical play and enjoyment I prepared a two course meal for imaginary friends. It took planning, hunting and gathering to fulfill the satisfaction of an impressive feast. Chinaberries were the main ingredient, followed next by small stones, small sticks broken into small pieces, and blades of luscious green grass. Put these flavorful ingredients together with a water base, simmered and stirred regularly on a pretend cooking stove; a wonderful soup was produced. The berries floated to the top making a stunning impression. Every good southern meal must have a dessert. Mud pies were a favorite to prepare. This recipe called for the darkest black dirt to be found, along with a little white sand, and red clay. Adding water swirled the ingredients together.  Hand mixing was a necessity with the fingers fully engaged to thoroughly combine the dirt and clay together.  More dirt may be added as needed to make a nice doughy type pastry.  Individual brown pies were patted out and laid side by side waiting for the crowning touch. Decorating the pies was done by adding a flower, small red or purple berries, or making a design with a small twig.  Now the meal was complete and must be served to the guests who were present – a dog, cat, doll, or turtle.  Imaginary friends would also show up, and were welcomed to partake of the meal.

Pretending and playing in the yard for hours on end, was great fun, but came with an added benefit.  Skills were being developed in creative cooking, and cake decorating, with a lingering desire to be of help to mother in the kitchen.  Even today as I challenge myself in decorating and creating, the playful, exciting energy goes right back to that splendid time as my spirit was awakening to imagination, curiosity and joy.

*~Kathy and Her Dog~*

## 8) Raw Head and Bloody Bones

It wasn't even Halloween,
When we traipsed between,
The first and second floor.
No other adventure would offer more.
Up the stairs we started,
Cousins that couldn't be parted.
Two rooms to explore, and a dusty old attic,
The corners so dark and dreary, you're likely to be frantic.
Aunt Hazel was there, tapping on our backs.
She had our attention and stopped us in our tracks.
Don't go up those stairs, she said exceedingly aloud,
You'll see Raw Head and Bloody Bones,
And to catch you they would be proud.
They snarl, they growl, long arms reach out and grab,
You may even see one lying down on a wooden slab.
Many are advancing; for if you choose to go,
Some of you may be missing, when the lights are getting low.
Little children are their favorite catch,
And they'll have you in a quick snatch.
Hearts were beating faster, eyes widely open and staring,
Our teeth began to chatter and we hugged each other pairing.
We scurried down the stairs screaming, and out the door with a
clatter.
We were out so fast, what came about next didn't even matter.
No upstairs adventure today,
Let's just stay outside and play.

~Cousins Playing: (from left to right) Matt & Spring Barney with Lindsey & Allison Cawley~

# 9) Say Pepsi Please

The "junk yard" was a favorite place Daddy explored on weekends when I was growing up during the 50s and 60s. On Saturdays he loaded his pickup truck with unwanted things to discard along large trash items that couldn't be burned in the barrel. A few useful items he found to bring home and some were treasures. I was intrigued when a large metal Pepsi sign appeared after his junk yard adventure. It was a large, tall sign that was used for road side or store advertising once upon a time. The sign was yellow with an eye catching bottle of Pepsi and the caption "Say Pepsi PLEASE" in large letters. Daddy's plan was to use the good piece of metal to give support to his outside building. He nailed it to the back of the "car shed" to support the old, aging wooden boards. During that period of time it was quite customary for country homes to have wooden car garages built separate from the house. Daddy's car shed had shelves built on either side to hold automotive items and odds and ends. Some of the car sheds were double for families that could afford two vehicles.

There were times the shed would be the perfect place to set up the grill for bar-b-queuing chicken on a rainy weekend. Animals took refuge from the rain and cold weather in the sheds. The large metal sign was perfect support in preserving the building, and was nailed out of sight on the back side. It seemed unjust to have the sign hidden from view with its vibrant color and clear message, but it was a little rusty and worn.

Have you ever seen another advertising sign with the word "PLEASE" engraved so largely? Saying "please" and "thank you" were phrases used regularly during a time when politeness and kindness was so highly valued and strictly taught by parents.
After my parents passed away, I took care in removing the sign from its place of slavery on the back of the shed. Honoring a precious memory seemed important. Its subtle message over the years seemed too personal to leave behind. An old sign like that would be of great value now, even in deterioration. It's worn face and telltale history is invaluable.

*~Metal Sign Retrieved From Back of Shed~*

# 10) Big Ma

## *The Prayer and Final Days*

There were five in our family - me, my parents, sister Rose and Big Ma (Lucy Poss). She lived with us from the day I was born. Here are a few fond memories.

* I Remember her happy smiles and laughs in abundance as she enjoyed her many birthdays when the family gathered to celebrate with food and loving gifts at the Lincolnton Clubhouse.

* The creaking sound of her rocking chair as she rocked by the fireplace in the winter.

* Early Christmas mornings when she joined us to see what Santa left by the tree. She rejoiced with us as we opened our gifts.

* A summer evening listening as she played her harmonica while we enjoyed time together on the front porch.

* The loving smack on Daddy's cheek as she kissed him before he left for work each morning, and every night before she went to bed.

* Playing Chinese checkers or a Rook card game for hours on a Saturday afternoon.

* Blowing kisses and waving out the window as I left the house each morning to wait by the road for the school bus.

* Homemade Bread Pudding made from left over biscuits and grits.

* Swaying back and forth in the swing under the shade tree while singing songs.

* Love for her "home" church, St. Paul Methodist, and her visits there periodically during the middle of the week.

* The walking cane (she referred to it as her stick) as she used it to give support in walking around the yard. It had other practical uses such as uncovering pecans nestled under a bed of autumn leaves.

## The Prayer

The most impressive memory was her bedtime prayer. Each evening I went to her room to watch TV with her or talk a little before she went to bed. One evening I skipped joyously to her room as I had many times. It was about 8:00 P.M. Her room was dark and the door partly open. I tiptoed as not to wake her if she was asleep. As I stood just outside her room, I overheard whispers and realized she was praying. I heard my name in her prayer and the names of other family members, even those we didn't see often. I felt humbled listening to her sweet, sincere and loving talk with Jesus. Even though I felt I was intruding in a most private moment, I was glued in my position. I was moved emotionally by that moment. Tears flowed down my cheeks. It was a revelation of what I always knew without a doubt. She loved her family deeply, each and every one. She wanted God to bless us all abundantly with love, joy and safety.

## Final Days

During the last few weeks of Big Ma's life, she was at home in her room bound by illness and pain. Care was provided by family members around the clock with devotion. In the last hours of life, she couldn't speak, but communicated by looking into our eyes and reaching out with her hand to touch our faces when we were at her bedside. She listened as we talked to her. I felt the love in her eyes and her touch. She was giving us one last message, and reassuring us that she was unafraid of the journey ahead. Big Ma left her legacy and imprinted our lives with deep love that still lingers in my heart, and brings joy with my every remembrance of time spent with her. I cherish her essence that remains as part of who I am.

*~Big Ma's Birthday Celebration at Lincolnton Clubhouse 1966~*

*~Big Ma is 87~*

*~Big Ma and Rose Mary Poss~*

# 11) Hometown Doctor

In times bygone, country doctors were few and local home visits were commonplace. During the 1930s, house calls accounted for 40 percent of physician interactions. Several days each week when doctor clinics were closed, they took to the road, traveling the community. In my hometown, Lincolnton, Georgia, we were served by just such a doctor. Doctor Pennington was the only doctor in town.

My grandmother, Lucy Cartlidge Poss ("Big Ma"), lived with us. Every so often Big Ma got to feeling poorly and Daddy had to make the call. Soon Dr. Pennington would appear climbing the porch steps with his shiny black medical satchel in hand. Sitting close by her bed, or near her rocking chair, he attended her every need.

Completing his exam, he'd saunter into the kitchen with his diagnosis for Mother and Daddy. As he finished his report, the conversation invariably turned to any number of subjects. If Mother were cooking, the good doctor always took note. He was happy to partake but was satisfied with leftovers; pride did not get in his way. Often it was a cold biscuit or piece of pie. One time I saw him pop a small raw onion in his mouth and eat it while talking. I cringed! I couldn't believe my eyes. In summer months he was interested in what Daddy had planted in our garden. He'd stroll through the garden rows picking tomatoes right off the vine and eating them on the spot. Dr. Pennington was not only our doctor but our family friend. Whenever he was ready to leave, after his house call, Daddy presented him with a paper sack filled with vegetables and goodies to take home. He continued to care for and call on Big Ma until 1968 when, at 88, she died at home in her bedroom.

Whenever anyone in my family was not up to snuff, an appointment was made with Dr. Pennington's clinic office. At three years old, I got the chickenpox. Unfortunately, it was a nasty infection near my navel. Mother drove me to Dr. Pennington's clinic where the doctor quickly determined that lancing was imperative. I was none too excited about the news and pending procedure. I was carried to the treatment room, thrashing and screaming. It took three people to hold down my tiny body so that the doctor could do his job. Clearly I survived but the event was scorched into my memory.

Another visit to the doctor's office and probably the most embarrassing was when I was five years old. Mother diagnosed an infestation of intestinal worms. This meant another visit to the doctor's office. I sat fairly calmly in the waiting room, but when my turn came, I dug in my heels into the floor and Mother literally had to drag me into the treatment room. I feared the worst. Would I have to undress so the doctor could look for the worms? As it turned out the doctor only wanted to inquire about the situation. I immediately calmed down and the treatment of medication took care of the problem.

Like many a child, I had my share of sore throats and colds and those were less frightening. Fevers kept me home from school and sent me to Dr. Pennington. The penicillin shot was tolerated because I knew there would be a reward. Afterwards while Mother was getting the prescription filled at the drug store around the corner, I could choose a comic book and get a fountain cocoa-cola with ice to take home. My favorite comic book was "Life with Archie" and "Betty and Veronica." I almost had an instant healing on the way home.

To me, Dr. Pennington was a very wise man and could fix anything that went wrong with our bodies. Clearly he was a close friend of Jesus for he was a savior in Lincolnton, Georgia. God bless Dr. Pennington, and others like him, who treated all our physical needs, calmed our mind and lifted our spirit as well. He was our hometown hero.

*~Dr. Weems Pennington, Sr.~*

# 12) Something in the Water

The "backed up" water of Soap Creek, in hometown Lincolnton, Georgia was just a short walk from our back yard. An amusing story Mother shared was a time she and Daddy took me on the fishing boat when I was barley walking. She laid an old quilt pallet on the bottom of the boat so I could play and nap. Fish caught were hooked on a metal chain that hung over the side of the boat. This kept them alive and fresh.

To keep me occupied they placed a small pole with fishing line and hook in my hands. Moving the pole from side to side I joyously splashed in the water. Surprisingly my erratic movements snagged a small fish. It was a complete surprise that I developed fishing skills so young. The small fish was taken off the line and released.

Fishing in the pond at Clyde Ivey's on Iveytown Road across the road from Mama Ivey's house was an exciting summer activity. The adventure began by digging for worms in the fertile soil and placing them in a tin can. Next was to find a pole with fishing line and a bobfloat. The pond was down a hill full of briars and grassy brush and could be dangerous. We used the buddy system when several cousins were visiting and made sure we were all safe. A carefree afternoon was not only for our entertainment, but was the hope of having fish for supper. It was fun competition to see who would catch the first fish and the biggest fish. One of the rules was to focus and stay still and quiet. A fish was more likely to bite under such perfect conditions. We caught fish, swatted gnats and received many mosquito bites on those muggy afternoons.

Another "fishy story" was at our home on Lori Court, Lexington SC. Feeding the turtles early on summer mornings was not only gratifying, but was an expected treat for the turtles. On a usual morning around 7:00 A.M., four of five turtles waited on the bank. With my appearance more swam over to partake of the feast. I called out, "Here turtle, turtle, come and get your treats". Many heard the call and the water became alive with ripples and activity as excited turtles rustled and raced to be the first in line to get a snack. Creek turtles have no interest in sharing with each other; they fight over the smallest of scraps. It was especially exciting to see new baby turtles that were no larger than a small fist. They too looked for a nibble. One morning of turtle feeding was not so usual. I was standing on the edge of the creek bank with the water just inches from my feet. I looked in the murky water and couldn't believe my eyes. There was a shape in the water that looked like a huge turtle with a shell that looked much larger than a dinner plate. It was motionless. Looking twice and shaking my head in disbelief, I became more curious. Could it be a huge rock on the bottom that I had not seen before? I bent over, closer to the water to look again into the murk, hoping that my vision would reveal the truth. As my eyes focused, I saw markings on the top of a shell that indeed was that of a turtle.

I then noticed the creature had a huge head that was haggard and pre-historic looking. As I realized the oddity of the moment, I feared this gigantic amphibian could come out of the water and take my hand into his mouth with one bite! Intuition took over, I straightened up, gasped and took a step back. I looked again and the creature had moved about two feet back and still on the bottom. The water swirled a bit and became somewhat cloudy but the now motionless turtle was still there. I reached for a nearby tree branch to poke in the water to confirm my finding. I looked again and the gigantic turtle had vanished! Did I really see a prehistoric creature? A gift indeed to experience a rare sighting of a very old alligator turtle (learning this after researching with Mr. Google) He may have lived in the waters of Twelve Mill Creek for ages. It was "the big one that got away". A creek monster it seemed for a moment. It was a glimpse of a rarity. What else is in the water?

*~Twelve Mile Creek~*

*~Alligator Turtle~*

# 13) Elsie

Large pretty eyes and a face of black and white,

That's Elsie the cow – a name given so trite.

She ran fast and wild and grazed on the grass.

At the fence she waited to see the day pass.

Horns developed on her brow,

And she tucked her head, sat on her knees as if to bow.

Friends right away with laughter and hugs,

She came behind me and curiously gave me a tug.

A big truck came and Elsie stepped in.

Sad tears rolled down my cheeks and goodbye seemed a sin.

Elsie, my friend, to market she will go,

Never again would I see her and I'd miss her so.

Small farmers depended on the earth,

Growing fruits and vegetables, and animal birth.

Money had to be made from the gift of the land,

No one gave a thought of a relationship so grand.

A loved friend is forgotten not,

Please don't let her be in someone's cooking pot!

*~Elsie the Cow~*

# 14) Sweetness of Life

The tender times of childhood are gone, but the sweetness of life lingers in memories of fun and carefree days. Family life in the country often revolved around small farming. Whether it was a vegetable garden, fruit trees or an assortment of cows, hogs and chickens, there were always children playing. Let's take a trip back to the 1950s and early 1960s.

### Beans & Tomatoes

Summer days were busy. To avoid the humidity and the hot afternoon sun, peas and butter beans were commonly picked in the early morn. Chairs were circled under a large shade tree as the family gathered round to shell the vine delights. With bowl in lap and hands busy, many a life problem was solved during conversation. News was discussed and neighborhood or town gossip perked curious, interested ears. Neighbors and family often stopped by and pitched in a helping hand.

A favorite chore was to run down to the tomato patch and hunt through the vines for the biggest, reddest tomatoes. Back at the house a large, galvanized tub was filled with water. Soon bright red tomatoes were bobbing up and down in the filled tub. They seemed to play and dance in the water, and seemed to say, "Pick me, pick me," as water clinging to their skin caused them to glisten and shine.

Peeling and cutting the tomatoes, in preparation for cooking, was long and arduous. After cooking, the tomatoes were put in canning jars or placed in plastic containers or clear bags to be frozen. It was important to have food put away for winter meals. The biggest and reddest tomatoes were saved on the windowsill for sandwiches and salads. Two slices of white bread, generously smeared with mayonnaise, a thick slice of tomato sandwiched between, salted and peppered to taste was a lunch-time delight.

### The Green Snake

In front of Mama Ivey's house, and near the dirt road was a huge oak tree with lots of shade from the hot summer sun. One day a pick-up truck was parked under the tree. The truck bed was a wonderful stage to play act, sing and dance. Cousins came over to visit and most times we were sent outside to play. Playing in the truck, passing automobiles stirred up dirt from the road coating us with a layer of dust. It was fun to jump up and down; waving our hands and hollering at passing motorists. Getting grimy was the least of our worries.

As we played an unannounced visitor joined us with a plop. It was a bright green garden snake that fell from the tree limbs above. As the green intruder wiggled at our feet, one might have thought we had been invaded by a king cobra. Screaming and squealing in terror, we scrambled out of the truck. Our ruckus was heard in the house. Curious adults soon ran out to see what the matter was. Amused by our over reaction, the snake was carefully removed to a safer place. Fear increased as this incident lead to shared snake stories and ghostly stories as well. Truth and fantasy lies side by side in the curious and impressionable mind of a child.

## The Cement Fish Pond

Mama Ivey had a little, hand made, circular cement pond in her front yard. It was little more than six or seven feet in diameter. It was a favorite past time to watch the goldfish swimming lazily in the water. Lovely yellow daffodils stood in near-perfect rows, extending across the yard. Often we lay on our stomachs with our heads hanging over the edge to peer into the pond. Our thoughts traveled to magical and wonderful places while looking at the reflections in the water. We shared thoughts and made up stories – fantasies of sharks, sea monsters and sailing in the ocean wide.

## Apples & Pecans

Two crab apple trees grew in our yard. I often picked ripe apples from the tree and even though very tart, I skipped around the yard enjoying a quick snack. Some years the apples grew in clusters causing the limbs to bend over low to the ground. When the apples were plentiful Mother made lots of homemade crab apple jelly. She stowed many a jar away for use in the winter days and the pretty glistening amber jars made desirable gifts for holiday gift giving. Tall and impressive, five pecan trees spread across our property. They usually produced a generous crop of pecans. Chilly autumn winds gusting through the trees, caused the limbs to sway, sending the ripened pecans plunging to the ground. Saturday or Sunday afternoons were the time when the family spent hours raking through the crisp, brown fallen leaves for the delicious nutty jewels. Two nuts held together in one hand and squeezed firmly, cracked the nuts for eating. There was always time to stop the hunting and enjoy a sweet, fresh delight.

## Contemplation

Mother Nature was my friend. I often felt that she called me to dance and play under the warm spring and summer sun, with skies of blue filled with wispy white clouds. Fearsome thunderstorms, laced with flashes of lightening brought much needed rain to nurture our land. Fragrant summer flowers pleased our senses and gave beauty and grace to our homes. Fall brought crisp, cool days and time to harvest the fruits of our labor. The winter brought rest and rejuvenation for Mother Nature. We, too, needed a rest – a time to consider in gratitude all that we had been given. The bounty of nature nurturing our spirit and soul is truly the sweetness of life.

*~Pecan Tree~*

# 15) Gardenias In the Graveyard

A feared place of final rest,

A trip to heaven in their Sunday best.

An iron fence old and rusted in a perfect square,

A gate wide open full of briars to beware.

Names and dates barely readable of someone's forgotten kin,

Deceased so young, could it have been a plight of sin?

Graves with cement covers, now broken and shifted,

In curiosity there was no wonder the top must be lifted.

A large Gardenia bush smack in the middle,

Sweet fragrance it gave much more than a little.

See the beauty of the Gardenia; take some home today,

Those buried here, what would they have to say?

As the fragrance of the Gardenia lingers long with sweetness,

Reverence the souls and pray they left with completeness.

# 16) The Harmonica

A cool breeze gave relief from the hot, humid mid-summer afternoon. We were on the front porch, Big Ma and I, enjoying a lazy and contented feeling. She swayed back and forth gently in her rocking chair. We noticed fragrant smells from the nearby Mimosa tree. We watched the delicate, soft pink blooms dancing in the breeze.

My thoughts drifted as I gazed at the large gardenia bush within sight; standing tall and florid in the middle of the cemetery across the highway. Its lovely aroma rode on the coat tail of the wind filling the air. Taking her harmonica in hand Big Ma rubbed it carefully with her apron to clean and shine it before lifting it to her lips. I was lured by the happy, carefree tunes; Big Ma tapped her foot and I leapt to my feet dancing around the porch.

Big Ma (Lucy Cartlidge Poss) lived with our family before I was born. She was a tall woman, wearing an apron around her waist as part of her everyday attire. The apron came in handy when finding treasures in the yard or collecting vegetables from the garden.

She placed the harmonica in the pocket of her apron, picked up her walking cane (she called it her "stick") and we left the porch for a walk. We often spent time outside sitting under the shade trees and walking around the yard. A favorite place was the swing hanging from a large limb of a huge oak tree. The swing creaked as we moved back and forth talking and laughing. We made our way back to the front porch to take another rest before going inside for the evening. She retrieved the harmonica from her apron pocket, smiled and lifted it to her lips playing, "What a friend we have in Jesus". Big Ma rarely attended church but her faith was sure. She sang church hymnals, prayed and kept her Bible near for reference and reading. The air felt heavy as we watched the sun tucking itself behind the clouds. Tomorrow will be another day for the merry melodies of the harmonica.

# 17) A Merry Mixture of Memories

Clothespins holding clean clothes on the line.  Take them down one at a time.

Bare feet on wooden boards of wooden porches.

Sand between your toes, and the smell of dirt after the rain.

Ironing board backed up to the sink to wash my hair with shampoo and cream rinse.

Stars sparkling in the night sky.  Lightning bugs buzzing by.

Licking cake batter from a wooden spoon.

Singing church songs while dancing barefoot in the grass.

Yellow watermelon cut in sections on the front porch steps.

Pink Mimosa blooms tickling your nose with sweetness of fragrance.

Getting scooted with the garden hose on a hot August day.

Mama Ivey's treat…Ritz cracker, peanut butter, topped with marshmallow and toasted.

I see the moon and the moon sees me.  God bless the moon and God bless me.

Looking into the water well, so dark and deep.  Need rain to make it complete.

Chickens clucking, eating bugs and cracked corn.

Stirring the pig slop in the tall bucket with Daddy's homemade wooden paddle.

Pigs running through the tall grass and wallowing in the mud hole.

Thunder storms, lightening, and rain pounding on the upstairs tin roof.

Gathering chicken eggs from the nest, brown ones and white.

Mules yoked together going round and round. Cane syrup in the making.

Pulling apples and eating fresh from the tree, crisp, tart and juicy.

Doodle bug, doodle bug, your house is on fire, and they scamper out of the sand.

Long sleeve shirt, gloves and a bucket – a blackberry picking we will go.

Attending family reunions and playing with many cousins.

Going to funerals and looking in the casket.

Picking crowder peas and putting them in a basket.

Playing in the snow so rare, and making ice cream with sugar and cream.

Holiday dinners with special china and table decorations.

A field of cotton with workers toiling from sun up till sun down.

Watching and poking the fire as paper trash burns in a big barrel.

Treasures Daddy found at the "Junk Yard".

Sweeping a dirt yard with a broom made of twigs.

Going to the outhouse; using thin Sears Robuck pages to clean up.

Riding the school bus….number 6 and 12.

Looking for 10 cents items to buy at the Dime Store.

Willingham's Country store with pot belly stove and hoop cheese.

A fireplace mantel decorated with holy and red berries.  Christmas smells of joy.

Big Ma's bread pudding made with left over grits and biscuits.

Afternoon rain showers, May flowers and the smell of freshly cut grass.

Big flaky buttermilk biscuits with butter and homemade blackberry jelly.

Lifting up a hen and gathering fresh laid eggs underneath.

Rabbits captured in the wooden rabbit box provides supper for tonight.

Learning to make a caramel cake and winning a blue ribbon at the county fair.

The smell and comfort of clean air dried bed sheets.

Enjoying an RC cola and moon pie at Uncle Frank's store.

Cornbread and buttermilk in a glass tumbler makes a complete meal.

*~Wooden Paddle Made by Pete Poss, Family Butter Churn~*

# 18) Searching

What is the meaning of life?

Am I drifting without a purpose?

I've searched in the east,

I've searched in the west; .

I didn't find my purpose there.

I've looked into the eyes of the old,

I've looked into the eyes of the new born baby;

I didn't find it there.

I listened to the wise and spiritual,

I called out to God, "Help me find my way."

I sat in the silence for a long while.

The answer came to me.

It was crystal clear,

It's an inside journey.

I open my heart and mind;

The searching is over,

The awakening has begun!

*~Speaking at Unity of Columbia~*

...and all along my
heart was searching
for what my soul
already knew...

~Alexa

# 19) Do Trees Need Hugs

Do you remember when people around the 1970s went around hugging trees? What in the world was that all about? Were they crazy?

The idea lingered and resonated with me in a way unclear at the time. During the 1990s I was at a church outing walking nature trails. A huge oak tree presented itself before us, seeming very old due to its immensity. Eight of us encircled the tree joining hands; moving in as close as we could to the tree to give it an exhilarating hug. I felt the energy of the tree. It was a heart to heart connection; a feeling of joy. I officially became a tree hugger that day.

One evening years later I had another "tree hugging" experience. I was sitting on the back deck of our home with my feet propped up on the railing. I was in a thoughtful and meditative state enjoying the peace.

My emotional state was of appreciation and thankfulness. It was momentary bliss. The moment contained a strong compelling notion for me to go out into the wooded area and hug a tree. It was a soft inner whisper, but drove me to get up from my chair. I walked into the woods and began hugging one tree, then two, then three. I was guided to the huge, tall, double trunk pine tree that was the closest tree to the house.

During my hug, I asked this tree what it was feeling. To my complete amazement, the tree gave me an answer. With a small, clear, permeating whisper in my mind, it said, "Power and strength." In my surprise, I questioned what I just heard. It wasn't audible, but a voice none the less, came through clear as anything. Excited, I went over to my favorite oak tree, hugged it and asked for a message. The tree answered with, "I have much gratitude and love". Again, the gratitude was directed to me, and I felt it with every part of my being. Earlier in the year we saved this tree. It was marked for removal, but we pleaded with contractors to save it when they were putting in new sewer lines for the town.

The experience was exhilarating and weird at the same time. I was communicating with those wonderful trees. Communication with nature is possible and real when we open our hearts and minds to the majesty of life.

Tree hugging has a very different meaning to me now. I discovered something deeper within myself. I connected with the life energy that is present in all things. The universe whispers. Are we listening and how shall we respond?

*~Kathy at Chimney Rock, NC~*

"Just go out and talk to a tree.

Make friends with it."

~Bob Ross

# 20) Seven Rings True

## *Life and Wisdom of the Oak Tree*

Her life began as she sprouted into a tender sapling, shallow in the sand and rock of Lexington, South Carolina. Barely noticeable she struggled to survive. Forest animals and other creatures trampled over her. She wanted to survive as every cell of her little being was gathering strength.

Rooted just three feet from the slow moving Twelve Mile Creek she noticed how it flowed gently and smoothly, other times brisk and rapid. The calming creek at her side became a friend. She was in awe of the majestic pine tree towering high above her tiny branches. It was strong and overwhelming with a large base and then splitting into two trunks with strength and power. Years went by; she too became a tall, beautiful tree.

Summers were glorious as she dressed in rich green with shiny leaves providing shade beneath her umbrella canopy. Basking in the sun by day was delightful, but the nights were exciting as the shade of darkness fell like a thin veil. In lighted pathways the animals begin to gather under the soft moon glow. Creatures and a variety of bugs and flying insects come out to the night party. Lightning bugs danced in the moonlight and sprinkled their light decorating the dark sky and tree branches. Opossums, raccoons, squirrels, snakes, foxes, and beavers also roamed in the misty night air.

Autumns offered the oak tree transformation into royal, rich color of warm yellows with gold tones. As seasons changed the oak tree faced many challenges. She was once marked for removal by contractors, but her life was spared at the last minute. Beavers ripped the bark from her trunk, and she became weaker. A lightning strike caused serious damage to her tree top. It's a wonder, but she managed to continue her vibrant life. A tree does not know what failure means and it is not an option. Survival is the only thought. Vibrant life, the only purpose.

The rings of a tree tell the age and give much information about a tree. The oak tree whispered, "There is more". There are hidden messages imprinted in the rings. Again she whispered, "There are seven important messages that grow with me and are a pattern for living". These lessons are gifts for ALL creatures and humans. It is now time to awaken and listen to the deeper voices of nature. These messages will ring true for you. Here is what she told.......
Seven Paths of Wisdom and Wonder.

1) LISTEN to the sounds around you and deep within your being. Sounds and voices, loud or as faint as a whisper come into our energy space all the time. The whispers inside us are voices of guidance, energy, love, and our true self expressing. Be in tune as you listen – to hear. It may be a feeling, an inner urging with no sound at all! But if you pause and enter the silence for a moment, your inner knowingness will guide you. Be still and know.

2) SEE the fullness of your life. Beauty is all around. See the greatness in yourself and in others. You have inner eyes of revelation and compassion. Your soul delights in seeing and knowing. You will see clarity when confusion and fear is released. Feel what you see in your heart of hearts. Be in harmony with the dance of the universe. See with acceptance, understanding and compassion. See with love expressing as you.

3) FEEL with the thermometer of your being. In high energy, we fly on the wings of health and happiness. If our feelings are low in energy, we may need to pay attention to the signs we receive and take better care of ourselves. Notice fear or pain whether physical, emotional or mental. We feel with our heart, mind and soul. Messages appear when we are in tune with our feeling thermometer. Let your thoughts go to your heart space, where your feeling resides. Trust inner knowing and intuition as your guide.

4) BREATHE in life! Breathe deep to cleanse, breathe gently into calmness. As you breathe be aware of the fragrances and aromas that linger. Let your breath center you with your source of being. Feel the breath, and appreciate its role in sustaining life. From creative source breathe in life and love. Take easy breaths of harmony and love.

5) ACKNOWLEDGE your soul living an earthly experience. You are part human and part divine. You are one with the one. Acknowledge your wondrous miracle of life. Go deep within yourself and ask the universe to guide. You are one of a kind and an important light to the world. You are here for your perfect unfoldment. Acknowledge and know.

6)  APPRECIATE everything. Thank you, thank you, thank you, calls forth the universe to sing the song of life with you. Appreciation is the soul's majesty, and is the human movement with energy. No matter how life shows up, it is the pleasure and nature of the soul to be humble and thankful. Celebrate. Appreciate.

7) LOVE with all your essence. All is love and love is all. The beginning with no end and in all the empty spaces in between. Love gives all, everywhere, all the time, and enfolds every cell and every breath. It is the harmonizer and healer.  It is
the glory of the most high vibration, and the whispers of the lowly. Love heals every fear. Love restores life and fills every particle of space. It is the allness, it is the nothingness. Love is the center of the universe and radiates with, into, and for all. Love is source, abundance, and comforter. Love hears and knows every thought. Love is our true nature. Love embraces all that we are. We are perfect as we stand in love. We are awake, alive, and move forward because love is our pure being, and moves us in a direction of yes and more. As light as a feather love drifts in the gentle breezes and so strong it penetrates the impenetrable. It is the whole, omnipotent, omnipresent. God is love, and love is God. In the end love is all there is.

*After Thoughts From the Author*

The tree finally gave in to her circumstances. The physical difficulties were too much to bear. Her life was well lived and she found me to witness her lifespan and to see and listen to her teaching. The stump stood many years more with life of its own until it too was taken by raging flood waters of 10-4-15. Memories linger and I miss my wisest teacher, a cherished friend and my refuge in the stillness. I will forever hold her whispers of wisdom in my heart. Seven rings true.

*~Notice How the Seven Center Rings Stand Out~*

## 21) What Christmas Means to Me

*As a Child.....*

Excitement as December approaches.

What gifts shall I ask?

Trimming the tree with lights, glitter and decorations.

The wonderful aroma as Mother bakes cakes and pies.

Special activities and church services.

Waking up early on a chilly Christmas morning.

Surprises under the Christmas tree.

Mother, Daddy, Big Ma, Rose and Me around the tree,

Singing Rudolph the Red-Nosed Reindeer with Gene Autry.

Dressing up for church in red, greens and gold.

Hugs, merry wishes, and good cheer from everyone.

Bible readings and the Christmas story.
God is love and gave us Jesus, the Christ child.

Singing Hark the Herald Angels Sing and Away In A Manger.

Eating and playing all day.

Cookies, candy and many food delights.

More love and fun in a day than ever imagined.

*As an Adult.....*

Enjoying the holidays to the fullest.

What gifts may I give?

Tree lights bright with a beacon of hope.

Cooking and baking with love as the main ingredient.

Participating and enjoying special activities at church,

A sanctuary for my soul.

My heart and soul singing songs of old that are renewed within my being.

Christmas day….the Christ is born in me, the hope of glory.

Delightful surprises given and received.

A piano recital with granddaughter playing Silent Night.

Seeing, knowing and feeling the Christmas spirit in everyone.

Reflecting and deepening my understanding of I AM.

My everyday song is Joy to the World.

Thankful for abundance everywhere and enjoying food, family and friends.

My love has grown and quickens my understanding,

I proclaim the great I AM and know peace for myself and all the earth.

*~Kathy and Santa Clause~*

*~1957 Coca-Cola Santa~*

# 22) Droplets of Wisdom

## *The Big Flood*

*(October 2015 - Lexington, SC)*

Water dams break even when they are deemed to be safe and secure.

Family, friends and neighbors are priceless.

Calling a 24/7 prayer line or praying with a friend in crisis centers us in the Divine.

Life situations and circumstances may change quickly, be alert.

Being prayed up heals hurts and strengthens the spirit to move forward.

Placing angels as symbols confirming the presence of God is comfort to the soul.

Acting quickly when intuitively guided is wise.

Hot water running through the faucet is a blessing.

A washer and dryer are better than a wooden wash board.

Removing mud from valued items is very different from playing in the mud.

Material items are just stuff.  Don't hold them too tight.
It's okay to talk to strangers when they walk up in your yard and ask if they may help.

Lots of hugs are needed when crisis comes.

Comforting messages are revealed at critical times if we but stop, look and listen.

Laughter really is the best medicine.

A hot shower or bath everyday is overrated.

Be willing to let go of "ought to be" and "should".

Living with less is more when appreciation kicks in.

A foundation of faith gives hope and courage.

The magic of love overrides the misery of loss and pain.

*~Kathy's Back Deck~*

*~Kathy's Home~*

## 23) Strange Sighting

The Old Mill Pond, named after the cotton mill over 100 years ago, was once a large, multi- acre pond in a beautiful, wooded setting. It was placid, serene and great for fishing and row boating. The flood of 2015 changed things. How sad to see a thriving, watery pasture reduced to a rippling stream coursing through many muddy acres with trees torn asunder.

On the frightful day of the flood we stood on our second floor deck watching a raging river. Once a small creek, now roaring waters flowed just below our feet and was surrounding our home. We stood helpless and in fear at an unbelievable sight. The rising water lifted our packed full 10" x 16" storage shed off its foundation and it began to float away as if it were a boat on an ocean wave being carried to a mysterious destination. Within seconds it turned in the direction of the water currents and floated behind trees and out of sight. Moments later a thunderous crash sounded and we knew our shed was no more. Scores of belongings swept away in a flash into what might as well have been a deep abyss.

Where had it all gone? Had any of it survived? Are our belongings buried in mud or maybe they floated downstream to submerge in the beautiful and huge Saluda River. Perhaps years from now adventure seekers will be out for a hike and discover some of the items. Gone was Rich's father's hand-made barrel chair, a box full of Christmas ornaments from many generations past. An antique wooden and leather love seat, souvenirs from vacations past, a shell collection, canning jars and flower vases. Years ago it had taken three men to carry the heavy, oaken workbench to the shed. It must have weighed several hundred pounds. There were countless tools, garden and lawn equipment and other large and small items too numerous to mention or remember; all gone to a watery grave.

Weeks after the flood, as we returned to some semblance of normalcy, we took walks around the area to survey the damage and observe the reconstruction efforts. While looking out over the muddy expanse of the Old Mill Pond we experienced a strange sighting. What was it, we wondered? A strange object dumped in mud that shouldn't have been there. It was red and mangled there in the center of the pond. Vandalized by nature's wrath, it had survived the onslaught. Something about that distant red object was familiar. We squinted bringing it more into focus. Could it be, there standing tall and battered? Yes, it was our red lawn mower!

It survived the tenacity of the storm. Astonished and amazed at the surprise we began to laugh. Sometimes reality is more laughable than fiction. For a moment we considered trying to rescue "Old Red," but practicality and safety dictated otherwise.

The sight was so weird that we were drawn back several times, always taking our camera. It was a little peculiar to feel an odd affection for a lawn mower. On one occasion we talked to others who were gawking at the sight. We had to share that we were the proud owners of that lawn mower. They laughed with us and we shared the light side of our somewhat sad story. It was fun taking the grandchildren to see a sight they will never see again but might remember and laugh about for decades to come.

   In a way our pride was tickled as we fantasized that "Old Red" had hung around long enough to say goodbye. A terrible event harbored a special memory to lessen our concerns and remind us that in the midst of tragedy spontaneous joy happens.

## 24) The Message

Our happy corner of the world is in Lexington, South Carolina, where Twelve Mile Creek flows 25 yards behind our home.

Saturday, October 3, 2015 was a day of awareness and preparation. Warnings called for heavier than normal rain—maybe torrential. As a precaution, we reinforced our back door, the only probable entry point for water with plastic, heavy tape, and sandbags. If water reached the door we had done all we could. Feeling a strong urge, I placed my cement garden angel outside the back door, one on the front porch and one at each stairway leading to our back deck. With my hand over my heart I whispered a prayer, "I just need a little extra help."

On October 4, 2015, at 1:30 A.M., I awakened with an uneasy feeling. Checking the back door I saw water creeping within 3 feet of the door. Soon, the unthinkable happened. The creek literally invaded our home, claiming our first floor. Fortunately, we were upstairs when the Gibson Pond Dam burst and sent a high-speed, high-pressure surge of water down stream. It hit our home with such violence that it blew our heavy steel door and frame out of the supporting wall into the house. Almost instantly five feet of muddy water inundated our downstairs, personal belongings tumbling about like breaking matchsticks. Whatever was in its path was damaged or totally destroyed.

Safe and physically unharmed, we watched morning light dawning, but not without emotional pain and confusion. Our calm, peaceful creek was transformed in the blink of an eye to a watery terrorist.

Several days after the flood, a demolition crew was at work, attempting to salvage some of our mud-covered personal belongings. Amazingly, a fair number of items, including delicate glassware, had survived, buried in slime and unbroken. I had forgotten about the angels for there was no sign of them. After several trips in and out of the house, a conscientious worker found my garden angel. While she had been placed outside the backdoor with barricades behind her, the force of nature had relocated her well into the interior of our home. Sadly, her praying hands had been amputated at the wrists. In a flash, sadness changed to joy as I received a message that I know was from God. It almost shouted: "She gave you helping hands!" Even in the midst of chaos and fear God kept us safe and away from harm. How wonderful to know my prayer the day before the flood had been answered. My special angel is now at our front entrance as a constant reminder that we are always loved, supported, safe, and divinely protected.

## 25) Who am I

I am here

I am now

I am a product of my yesterdays

I am the potential of my future

I am a child of God
I am love

I am joy

I am peace

I am all that God is

I am God's eyes, hands and feet

I am the storm within myself

I am the calm of the storm

I am a bundle of emotions expressing in this human form

I am a spiritual being that existed before

I am anything and everything I wish to be

I am the thirst in the night

I am the water that quenches the thirst

I am a creator

I am the color of the rainbow

I am no color at all

I am the giver and the receiver

I am the teacher and the student

I am the life of God that lives and breathes

I am the small and silent thought of God

I am the all in everything

I am the whisper of nothingness

I am that I am, forever and always

# Acknowledgement

The following individuals contributed their time, support, inspiration and knowledge during the writing of my book. Thank you………

Matthew Barney, my son and Editor, for your expertise in formatting and publishing Amazon-Kindle eBooks and for your ideas and suggestions in arrangement of text and pictures.

Rich Little, my husband and friend, for your ideas, encouragement and editing skills in many of my stories.

Tom Poland, friend and author, for your support, encouragement and guidance in teaching me better ways to use grammar, how to write for publication, and editing some of my stories.

Margie Taylor, Catherine Senterfeit, Mary Ann Hutcheson, and Susan Merrill, for listening to me with support and love during our laughter therapy lunches.

There have been many others, too numerous to mention, who inspired me as well. Thank you for touching my life and making my journey a richer one.

*~Mary Ann (Sister Mary), Margie (Tweety Bird's Mother), Kathy (Spider Woman)~*

**More Pictures**

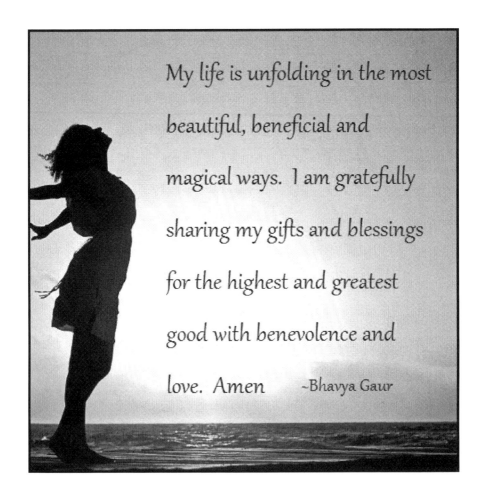

My life is unfolding in the most beautiful, beneficial and magical ways. I am gratefully sharing my gifts and blessings for the highest and greatest good with benevolence and love. Amen     ~Bhavya Gaur

*~Pete, Clotilde & Kathy Poss~*
*Ivey Reunion 1952*

*~Kathy and the Potty~*

**MAKE TELEVISION APPEARANCE**                    (Photo by Morgan Fitz)

A group of youngsters the Bethany Methodist Church in their first television appearance Saturday, Channel 12. Ranging in ages from 3 vocal numbers on the program of Directed by Mrs. J. C. Rowland, summer. Shown are (l-r, front row): Holloway, Connie Dukes, Gloria Booth, Barry Spence, Perry Rowland, Norman Talbert; (second row): Kathy Poss, Judy Banks, Bob Cooper, Sandra Jones, Forrest Spence, Ellen Teasley, Roger Teasley; (third row): Travis Reed, Melinda Teasley, Sandra Talbert, Gloria Partridge, Tony Rowland, Alicia Reed, Dean Cooper; (fourth row): Sarah Teasley, Gregg Booth, Jane Talbert, Shelby Jean Jones, Beverly Teasley, Patsy Saggus, Patsy Booth and Gail Burgess.

# ~TV Appearance, Bethany Church Children's Choir 1956~

THE AUGUSTA CHRONICLE-HERALD

Sunday, December 9, 1956

**MAKE TELEVISION APPEARANCE**—A group of youngsters from the Sunday school at the Bethany Methodist Church in Lincoln County, Ga., made their first television appearance Saturday over WRDW-TV, Channel 12. Ranging in ages from 3 to 10 years, they presented vocal numbers on the program of Mary and Fargo Pope (l). Directed by Mrs. J. C. Rowland, the group was formed last summer. Shown are (l-r, front row): Tony Booth, Bill Partridge, Lily Holloway, Connie Dukes, Gloria

(Photo by Morgan Fitz)

Booth, Barry Spence, Perry Rowland, Norman Talbert; (second row): Kathy Poss, Judy Banks, Bob Cooper, Sandra Jones, Forrest Spence, Ellen Teasley, Roger Teasley; (third row): Travis Reed, Melinda Teasley, Sandra Talbert, Gloria Partridge, Tony Rowland, Alicia Reed, Dean Cooper; (fourth row): Sarah Teasley, Gregg Booth, Jane Talbert, Shelby Jean Jones, Beverly Teasley, Patsy Saggus, Patsy Booth and Gail Burgess.

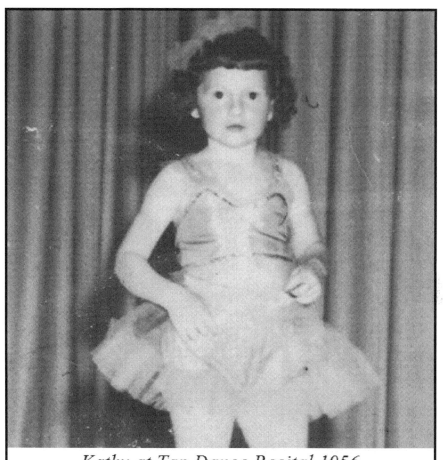

*~Kathy at Tap Dance Recital 1956~*

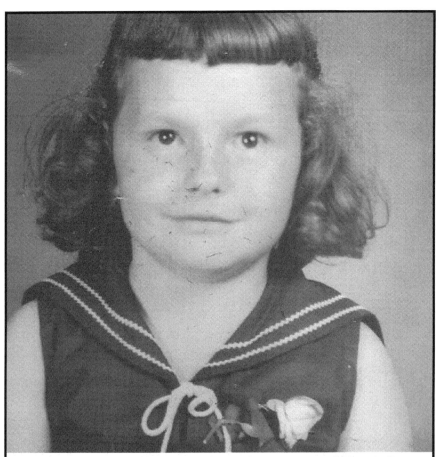

*~First Grade Picture (Big Ma pinned the white rose on Kathy's top that morning)~*

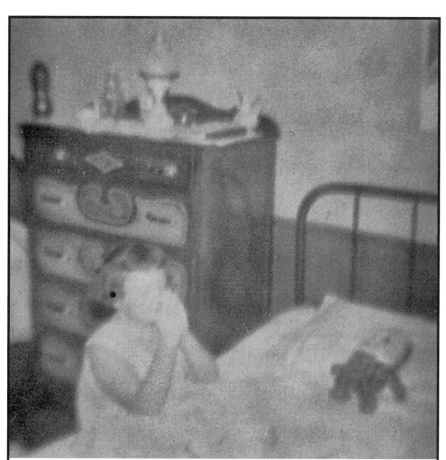

*~One God and Father of All, Who is Above All,*
*and Through All, and in You All~*
*Ephesians 4:6*

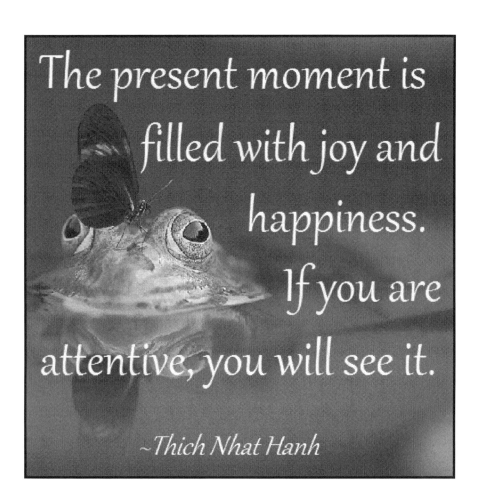

The present moment is filled with joy and happiness. If you are attentive, you will see it.

~Thich Nhat Hanh

*~Lincolnton Red Devils (Kathy on far left)*
*Homecoming 1966~*

*~The Poss Family 1966~*

*~Kathy 1970~*

*~1973, Back: Kathy & Paul Barney, Rose Mary Poss, Front: Hope, Clotilde & Pete Poss~*

*~Kathy with Spring & Hope 1976~*

*~Kathy, Paul, Hope Barney 1974~*

*~Kathy with her Mother in 1979~*

*~Paul & Matt in 1979~*

*~Spring, Matt, Kathy & Hope~*

*~Spring & Hope~*

*~Left to Right:  Matthew, Kathy, Spring and Hope in 1980~*

*~Matthew Barney with Kathy 1982~*

*~Rich & Kathy's Wedding Day July 14, 1985~*

*~Left to Right:  Kathy, Matt, Hope, Spring and
Richard A. Little~*

*~Left to Right: Rich, Hope, Kathy, Spring & Matt~*

*~Dress Up Time~*

Heart
Strings
Never
Break

*~Kindall Jackson and Faith Driggers~*

*~Damsi the Damselfly~*

*~Faith and Kindall~*

*~Rich & Kathy 2013~*

*~Kathy at Dollywood~*

*~Sabastian the Oak Tree~*

Pho.to Lab app.

*~Appreciating the snow 2014~*

*~Geese in Twelve Mile Creek~*

*~Rich & Kathy at Shag Club~*

**THE END**

Made in the USA
Middletown, DE
04 November 2023

41846666R00076